Empath
The Empath's Complete Survival Guide – 7 Steps To Self-Protection, Emotional Healing And Building Better Relationships As A Highly Sensitive Person

-2nd Edition

SUZANNE EVANS

DEDICATION

To all the empaths. You make the world a better place.

CONTENTS

INTRODUCTION

Welcome to the second edition of "Empath: The Empath's Complete Survival Guide – 7 Steps To Self-Protection, Emotional Healing, And Building Better Relationships As A Highly Sensitive Person".

This updated edition contains:

- The original 7 steps to self-protection, emotional healing and building better relationships.
- 8 new visualizations and guided meditations for empaths.
- New grounding techniques for empaths and the medical research behind how grounding works.
- The research behind the 7 healing steps, and how you can incorporate them into your daily life.
- 5 essential crystals for empaths.
- New information on the discovery of what could be considered the "empath gene" and what this means for empaths.
- The surprising results of brain scans of highly sensitive people in reaction to stranger's emotional states - and how this discovery impacts how empaths relate to themselves and the world.

I hope that you, like readers before, will gain benefit from this book. This edition, like the first, contains proven steps and strategies on how to survive and even thrive in the world as an empath.

If you are overwhelmed by other people's emotions, feel deeply, or are drained by everyday interactions then this book is for you. Likewise, if you already have strategies in place to protect yourself and are looking for more approaches on emotional healing or building better relationships, then this book will help you get there.

You may even be questioning whether or not you are an empath or highly sensitive person. This book will help you answer that question and give you more information on the characteristics, benefits, and challenges of being an empath.

If you follow the steps in this book you will experience emotional healing, less stress and anxiety, and a more balanced relationship with others and with yourself. You can start using these steps today, and you'll see profound benefits in your life. Warm wishes on your empath journey.

-Suzanne Evans

CHAPTER 1: AM I AN EMPATH?

Do you feel deeply? Have you often found yourself overwhelmed by other people's emotions? Do you sometimes take on other people's illnesses, troubles, or emotions? Have you ever felt completely drained by the emotional overload from a person or a situation?

Have you ever wondered – am I an empath? How can I protect myself and stop feeling so overwhelmed and drained? How can I heal myself and have beneficial relationships?

You've taken the first step to answering these questions by opening this book. The next step is exploring what an empath is, and whether or not you are an empath.

You may already have an inkling that you are an empath. Perhaps some of these statements are familiar:

- You have been told that you are too sensitive.
- You can feel emotions more strongly than most – of people, places, animals or objects.
- You are a sponge for other people's emotions or ailments.
- You are drawn to the healing or helping professions.
- You have a love of art, music or nature.
- You are curious about alternative or energy therapies.
- You feel more drained than most by negative environments.
- You feel deeply.

Perhaps some of these traits have led you to this book, to discovering whether you are an empath, and what being an empath means for you.

I have known many empaths that leave themselves open to negative relationships, draining environments, and stimulus overload. This has a negative effect on their emotional and physical health and their family, friend, and work relationships. It begins in early childhood, when empaths sense that they are different or more sensitive and able to see, hear, feel or know things that others don't. But there is no guide, no societal wisdom for empaths in our over-intellectualized society. Because of this, many empaths learn early on to push away their differences, deny their intuitive nature, or tend toward self-destructive behaviors such as co-dependency, non-existent boundaries, or self-numbing through drugs, medication or over-eating.

Through years of research, study and practice I have developed practices that allow empaths to embrace their gifts and thrive in the world. They can deflect psychic vampires, spot toxic relationships, and protect themselves from negative energies, while still bringing the gift of a compassionate, caring empath to the world. My hope is that this book will help you discover self-protection, emotional healing, and healthy relationships.

As the poet Jennifer Welwood eloquently wrote, "Each condition I flee from pursues me, each condition I welcome transforms me and becomes itself transformed into its radiant jewel-like essence."

* A note about Highly Sensitive Persons (HSPs) as described by psychologist Elaine Aron. HSPs have a low tolerance for stimulation from light, sound, smell, touch, taste, crowds, and more. Their nervous system is more sensitive or hyper-reactive to external stimuli and takes longer to calm down. An HSP is very similar to an empath, and they share many traits, especially in their heightened awareness of external environments. Many empaths are HSPs and many HSPs are also empaths. However, empaths not only feel stimuli deeply, such as emotions or energy of an environment, they also tend to take it on as their own. This is a step beyond the typical HSP. Knowing this, the survival tips in this book will work for both empaths and HSPs. Likewise, the

scientific research, discussed later in this chapter, is applicable to both HSPs and empaths.

What Is An Empath?

The simplest definition of an empath is one who feels deeply. But an empath is much, much more. An empath can feel deeply *and* take on the emotions, feelings, pain, and illnesses of surrounding people, and even environments. Empaths can feel other people's emotions as if the emotions *were their own emotions*, they can feel other people's physical pain as if it were *their own pain*. The feeling can persist even after leaving that person or that environment, as if the empath has taken on that emotion, or pain as their own.

An empath is like an emotional conduit. The empath can conduct emotional energy like copper conducts electricity. A narcissist, (the opposite of an empath on the emotional spectrum) is like an emotional insulator, they stop conduction like a piece of plastic or rubber. The narcissist has limited ability for emotional conductivity, while the empath has a natural, and immense ability to feel.

Just as there are many different types of flowers, trees, or animals – there are different types of empaths. No empath will be the same or have the same experience. Indeed, there is a wide spectrum of empaths and a continuum of sensitivity.

Some empaths are most sensitive to the physical ailments of others, taking the ailments on as their own. Other empaths are more sensitive to emotional states (people, environment, or objects) and take the emotional states on. Still other empaths are extremely intuitive and can have profound insight or intuition through dreams, premonitions, or other means. You may have one, a few, or all of these empath traits and abilities.

As you can imagine, being an empath comes with many benefits, but also many struggles. Before exploring these, take this survey to determine whether or not you are an empath.

Empath Questionnaire

1. I easily feel the pain or worries of other people, even strangers. (True/False)
2. I feel a deep need to restore myself in nature. (True/False)
3. Loud noises, odors, and other external stimuli bother me more than others. (True/False)
4. People with problems are pulled to me. I have been told that I am "easy to talk to." (True/False)
5. I frequently need time alone to re-center and recharge. (True/False)
6. I have strong intuition and rely on my intuition frequently. (True/False)
7. I prefer one-on-one interactions to large groups. (True/False)
8. My feelings are easily hurt. Sometimes I feel that I am too sensitive. (True/False)
9. I can easily feel other people's emotional states. (True/False)
10. Sometimes I feel that I absorb other people's emotional states. (True/False)
11. I can feel the emotional energy of places, environments, and large gatherings. (True/False)
12. I easily get overwhelmed in relationships (romantic, family, or friend), and feel that I lose myself to other people's emotions, needs, illnesses, or demands? (True/False)

How did you do? Did you find that you answered true to a majority of the questions? If so, you are most likely an empath. All of the above questions are traits of an empath. If you answered only a few as true, you may or may not be an empath. However, this book will still be of help in understanding the empaths in your life (there is at least one!).

The Empath – Nature Or Nurture?

Many empaths wonder how it is they came to be an empath. There are two different theories: nature versus nurture. Based on the nature theory, the empath trait is genetically passed down to the offspring from the mother or father. This is reflected in the world when a highly sensitive or empath parent has a highly sensitive or empath child.

Nature – The Empath Gene

A new study in the Journal of Neuroscience[1] from the University of British Columbia and Cornell University found a gene associated with a person's depth of emotional experience and sensitivity to emotional landscapes. Some people carry this gene variation and other people do not. Just as some people have a gene for brown eyes and others do not.

Those who have this gene variation – known as ADRA2b – have heightened sensitivity to external emotional stimulus and a much more intense response to emotional states – both positive and negative emotions. The researchers stated that people with this genetic variation have a more vivid perception of the emotional environment, greater emotional enhancement of memory, and heightened amygdala activation after emotional events (the amygdala is responsible for the fight or flight response).

This recently discovered genetic variation highlights how people differ in their sensitivities to emotional landscapes, and may be a genetic basis for HSPs and empaths.

Nurture – Early Life Events

Based on the nurture theory, a person would become an empath because of an external event. Research has shown that trauma before the age of 7 can influence a person's sensitivity level or susceptibility to chronic disease.

The CDC-Kaiser Adverse Childhood Experiences Study or ACE study had more than 17,000 participants (the largest study of its kind) and tracked how childhood trauma effected emotional and physical health as an adult. Brain imaging of people with childhood trauma shows alteration in the structure and function of areas in the brain responsible for memory, learning, and emotion.

---

1 Todd; Ehler et al. Neurogenetic Variations in Norepinephrine Availability Enhance Perceptual Vividness; Journal of Neuroscience 22 April 2015, 35 (16) 6506.

This may lead to hypersensitivity to other's emotions, other's pain/illness, body language and environment.

Beyond trauma, research on HSPs and empaths suggests that heightened sensitivity can arise from premature delivery, complicated pregnancy, low birth weight, or other environmental factors.

The majority of research does suggest that empath ability is most likely genetic, and environmental factors can either encourage or discourage the strength or activation of that gene/trait.

The Science Of The Empath Brain

A new study[2] using functional Magnetic Resonance Imaging (fMRI) confirmed through brain imaging that HSPs (Highly Sensitive Person) neural systems are engaged more strongly (than non HSPs) by other people's emotions. The part of their brains that were activated more strongly were responsible for awareness and empathy.

The study looked at HSPs brain activity in relation to emotions of the person's romantic partner *and strangers*. The emotions studied included: compassion, energy, excitement, friendship, joy, love, passion, pride, anxiety, fear, hurt, and sadness. The HSPs showed a very high level of empathy and awareness for all emotional states for both the romantic partner *and* the strangers. This finding, that HSPs brains activate at a much higher than average degree to other's emotions (positive or negative, loved one or stranger) may or may not be surprising to the empaths of the world.

Science is finding what many empaths have known for their whole lives - empaths have greater awareness and sensitivity to their world - loved ones and strangers alike. Empaths *feel*.

Benefits Of Being An Empath

---

2 Acevedo, & Aron, et. al. The highly sensitive brain: an fMRI study of sensory processing sensitivity and response to others' emotions. Brain Behav. 2014 Jul;4(4):580-94.

Being an empath is a great gift. You feel your world deeply, and your experience of the world is a beautiful multitextured, multicolored mosaic. You also connect with people deeply and can have truly intimate and meaningful relationships. You have great intuition, and an innate ability to heal yourself and others.
An empath's ability to connect and heal cannot be rivaled. This is why empaths are so frequently drawn to the healing professions and why they do so well in the healing arts. In fact, many studies show that empathy is a key factor in preventing burnout in the healing professions – empathy is protective for nurses, physicians, caretakers, and more.[3]

Empaths are also drawn to creative endeavors, preferring to express their deep emotions through music, writing, or artistic activities. The empath's ability to feel, listen, hear, and truly understand is a gift to the empath and to the world. The world is a better place because empaths bring their understanding and healing to the people in their lives.

Empaths make wonderful friends, mates, and family members. They are kind, compassionate, and loyal. They are excellent at reading people, situations, and events. Empaths also have a deep respect for nature and animals, which aligns with their desire to heal and protect.

It is estimated that 2-3% of the population are empaths, and 15-20% are Highly Sensitive People (interestingly, more than 100 species in the animal kingdom have highly sensitive members in their ranks). Think back on history, perhaps you can recognize some famous empaths? Gandhi, Mother Theresa, Siddhartha, Harriett Beecher Stowe, Chopin, Florence Nightingale, St. Francis of Assisi, George Orwell, and Helen Keller. There are so many notable people in human history that have felt deeply, and in doing so have cared for others, fought for others, healed others, and/or built beautiful art reflecting the depth of human emotion. Be proud to be an empath. Your contribution to this world is deep and meaningful. Remember, letting your own light shine gives others permission to do the same.

3 Bérangère Thirioux, et al. Empathy Is a Protective Factor of Burnout in Physicians: New Neuro-Phenomenological Hypotheses Regarding Empathy and Sympathy in Care Relationship. Front Psychol. 2016; 7: 763.

Challenges Of Being An Empath

Every coin has two sides, and just as being an empath has its positive side, it also has challenges.

Empaths feel deeply. Yes, something can be both a blessing and a challenge. Because empaths feel deeply, situations can hurt more and cause more stress. At times, being an empath without self-protection can harm your health or well-being.

Empaths are sensitive. Sometimes, it seems, too sensitive. This is related to feeling deeply. Empaths tend to internalize criticism, emotions, and situations that other people would brush off.

Empaths are magnets for people with problems and for energy vampires. Empaths tend to attract people with troubles. This causes an emotional and physical drain on empaths and can harm their health and well-being.

Empaths may have a hard time forming intimate romantic relationships. Some empaths have a fear of getting too close with another person. They find that sometimes in relationships their core self is lost or subordinated to the emotions, feelings and desires of their intimate partner. They have a hard time separating their emotions from their partner's emotions.

Empaths can become emotionally or physically ill from taking in too many emotions or pain from their surroundings. Panic attacks, depression, social anxiety, fatigue, and chronic health concerns can all result from empath overload.

These challenges highlight why it is essential for empaths to learn the skills in this book. With the proper techniques and lifestyle in place, empaths can survive and thrive – and bring their unique and wonderful gifts to the world.

This book will lead you into uncharted territory, to self-discovery and personal transformation. You are invited to be honest, flexible, and curious – but most of all, be compassionate toward yourself. There can be no flower without the mud. This book will be a guide, but you are your own best teacher. Practice, experiment and explore. Your own inner voice will let you know what is working for you.

Here are a few points to remember as you make your way on this journey:

- You will learn various techniques and principles of thriving as an empath. As best as you can, experiment and explore as you integrate them into your life. Practice and try the techniques more than once. Be your own teacher.
- Rough waters will come. Difficult emotions and self-judgment are bound to arise when we change our patterns of behavior. This book will help you build the resources and the emotional capacity to approach these difficulties.
- If your emotional cup is full, allow yourself to pull back and re-engage when it feels right.
- If the steps in this book are a struggle, allow yourself to take your time. Go slow. Show yourself compassion as you seek growth.
- During this book, treat yourself with kindness, understanding and care - as you would a friend. The inner critic can say harsh, cruel things that you would never say to a friend. Be your own best friend and let go of that voice.
- Approach this book mindfully. This means we can approach what we are feeling without pushing it away or holding on to it too tightly. Practice acceptance. As Donna Faulds wrote, "love not judgment, sows the seeds of tranquility and change."

CHAPTER 2: EMPATH INVENTORY

Being an empath impacts your relationships, your career, your health, and your well-being – indeed, every area of your life. You know what an empath is, as well as the benefits and challenges of being an empath. Before you learn the steps of surviving as an empath, take an inventory of your current situation. As Carl Rogers said, "The curious paradox is when I accept myself just as I am, then I can change."

Go to a quiet place and take the time to answer these questions as fully and truthfully as you can. Be curious, explore, and be honest with yourself. This inventory will help you know which areas of your life as an empath you need to heal, which relationships you need to work on, and which survival steps you will want to concentrate on most.

1. Make a list of the people who nurture you and the people in your life who drain you. People who nurture you will bring positive feelings to your life: peace, happiness, joy, love, and contentment. After interacting with these people, you will have a sense of well-being. People who drain you will leave you feeling tired, or with unsettled or negative emotions: anxiety, agitation, frustration, anger, depression, and low self-worth.

Examples of common relationship drainers are narcissists, constant complainers, gossips and drama queens, hypochondriacs, victims, and people who put you down or erode your self-worth. After interacting with these people, you will have a reduced sense of well-being. You will want to increase and nourish your interactions with people who nurture you. You will want to discontinue or set boundaries in the relationships that drain you. We will explore how to do this in the following chapters.

People Who Nurture Me:

People Who Drain Me:

2. Write a paragraph on your current overall emotional health. Note any and all people, environments, activities or situations that have a recurring or strong impact on your emotions. Be thorough.

3. Write a paragraph on your current physical health and well-being. Note any people, environments, activities or situations that have a recurring or strong impact on your health.

There is clear scientific evidence that chronic stress, anger, frustration, anxiety, depression, and other emotional states have a profound impact on your health and your risk for disease. It is extremely detrimental for an empath to take in other people's negative strong emotions/pain/feelings of illness. Be thorough in identifying people, environments, and situations that have a strong impact on your health.

Now that you have completed your empath inventory you are ready to apply the 7 survival steps to your life.

CHAPTER 3: CLEANSING RITUALS FOR EMPATHS

First thing first. Clean yourself and clean your environment. Remember the tradition of spring cleaning? The airing out of what is old and the letting in of what is new? Old energy and emotions can stick around, just like dust and grime. Empaths can collect this emotional "dust". So, first thing first, set the intention that you are ridding yourself and your environment of old energies and old emotions. Different traditions have different ways of doing this, here are two simple ways of cleansing.

1. Take an Epsom salt bath. Epsom salts are wonderful for clearing negative energies and negative emotions. Draw a warm bath and pour in one to two cups of Epsom salts. Set the intention that this bath will clear away any stagnant or negative emotions. Soak for 15 minutes. In the future, take an Epsom salt bath any time you feel like you need to be cleansed of negative or stuck energies.

2. Clear your home by burning sage. Use a sage smudging stick to clear your home of accumulated energies. Start at the front door. Light the smudge stick and gently wave the stick to spread the sage essence through your home. Move in a clockwise direction through all the rooms of your home. Pay particular attention to the corners. When you are finished extinguish the stick in a bowl filled with sand or salt.

In the following chapters you will find seven vital steps to follow for surviving and thriving as an empath. You may use only one and experience great results or use them all to great benefit. It will depend on your personal goals, experiences, and your own preferences and life situation. I encourage you to try each step multiple times and in varying situations. Be patient with the process and with yourself and know that you can always begin again.

CHAPTER 4: STEP 1: HOW TO USE SHIELDING & GROUNDING FOR PROTECTION

Shielding Visualization

One of the most important skills an empath can learn is known as shielding. Many psychologists and other mental health professionals recommend this technique to reduce emotional overload, or emotional "flooding". This visualization technique is critical in protecting yourself from taking in the unwanted emotions, pain, or illnesses of others.

Shielding involves visualizing a boundary or shield around your body. You may want to get a piece of paper and colored pencils for this exercise.

Begin by imagining or drawing a shield shaped like an oval or egg around your body. Be certain that it wraps around or shields your entire person. Imagine or draw the shield's color, thickness, and texture. Visualize whether it is warm or cold, and what it feels like. Imagine or draw the shield in as much detail as you can.

Now imagine that you are able to send out emotion and feelings through the shield. You are able to receive positive emotions and positivity through the shield. But *no* harmful or negative emotions or negativity can pass through the shield. The shield protects you completely. It blocks all negative emotions. It blocks all negative intentions. It blocks all harm. Use this shield whenever you feel the need, and in any situation where you are dealing with a person or environment that is draining or negative.

Now that you have drawn on paper or in your mind a detailed version of your shield you can follow this meditation on a daily, or as needed basis. It is an essential skill for empaths.

Shielding Meditation

- Find a quiet, comfortable place to sit where you will not be disturbed. Sit in a way that is comfortable, and that you can remain in for five minutes: cross-legged, upright in a chair, or kneeling on a cushion.
- Take a few slow, easy breaths. Relax and let go of any tension, thoughts or burdens that you are carrying.
- Let your eyes gently close.
- Notice your breath wherever it feels most comfortable. The air coming in through your nose, or the rise and fall of your abdomen, or in the gentle movement of your body. You do not need to change your breath, only notice it, as it rises and falls, in and out, like the movement of the sea. Stay in the moment of your breath. Feel the sensation of breathing and let go of any thoughts and any tension.
- Your mind may wander. Don't worry. When your mind wanders, gently guide it back to your breath.
- Move into your breath. Sink into it. Notice how it supports you and nourishes you without you having to do anything. Let your body breathe, while you feel the rise and fall of your breath.
- Now, bring to mind a beautiful shield of glowing light surrounding you. It covers you completely in its protective embrace.
- Its glowing color protects you. Inside it you are warm, safe, cocooned. Inside are feelings of love, and warmth, and your breath. The gentle rise and fall of your breath inside the safety of your glowing light.
- May you be happy.
- May you be healthy.
- May you be safe.
- May you live your life with ease.

- You are protected within your shield. Its glowing light surrounds you.
- Breathe.
- Gently, and when you are ready, let your shield fade. It can always come back whenever and wherever you need it. You only need to call it into your mind's eye.
- Now, and again, feel your body breathe. Feel yourself moving on the rise and fall of your breath.
- Relax.
- Slowly let the room and your surroundings come back into your awareness.
- Let your thoughts and feelings be just as they are.
- Slowly and gently open your eyes.
- Thank yourself for taking the time for self-protection.

The phrases in the above meditation "may you be happy, may you be healthy, may you be safe, may you live your life with ease" are based on loving kindness meditation. Loving kindness meditation is a practice of compassion for oneself and others. Tenzin Gyatso, the 14th Dalai Lama said, "caring for others requires caring for oneself." Self-care and compassion is vitally important for empaths.

Physical Shielding

Beyond visualizing your shield, you can also shield yourself physically. This technique is easy and effective in preventing people from draining you or from taking on other people's emotional states.

To physically shield yourself:

1. Cross your legs at the ankles.
2. Lock your fingers together and place your hands over your solar plexus (on your abdomen, slightly above your belly button).

This technique is especially beneficial in negative or emotionally toxic interpersonal interactions.

Physical Grounding/Earthing

The Earth's surface is continuously renewing its free electrons through the "global atmospheric electric circuit".[4] The surface of the Earth is electrically conductive. Electrons in antioxidants are known to neutralize the body's immune responses and regulate cortisol/stress reactions. Through direct contact with the Earth's surface (for example, walking barefoot) the Earth's electrons are able to enter the body and provide immense benefit.

Recent medical research has focused on the health benefits of grounding. People in the majority of studies were divided into two groups (known as randomized controlled trials): one group received grounding, the other received "sham" grounding, yet neither group knew whether they were receiving the grounded treatment or not. In all the studies, grounding had a significant and positive impact. Studies included earthing/grounding treatment for: sleep disturbances, chronic pain, stress, high cortisol/stress hormone levels, tension, glucose regulation, immune response, and osteoporosis.[5]

What is most relevant to empaths are the studies that show grounding significantly reducing stress. The studies showed grounding of 30 minutes to reduce stress, reduce heart rate and blood pressure, regulate stress hormone levels, reduce activation of electrophysiological properties in the brain, and activate the parasympathetic nervous system (the calming/rest system).

When you feel overwhelmed by emotions, in turmoil, or are experiencing emotional overload grounding can literally "bring you back to Earth". It will reduce your stress response, calm you, and amazingly, help your body heal or prevent degenerative disease. For an empath, grounding is an essential practice.

4 Williams E, Heckman S. The local diurnal variation of cloud electrification and the global diurnal variation of negative charge on the Earth. *Journal of Geophysical Research*. 1993;98(3):5221–5234.
5 Earthing: Health Implications of Reconnecting the Human Body to the Earth's Surface Electrons. J Environ Public Health. 2012; 2012: 291541.

There are a few different means of grounding:

1. **Go barefoot outside.** Go to an outdoor space, remove your shoes and socks and plant your feet firmly on the ground. Sit with your feet and skin of your body connecting to the Earth's surface, be it grass, rocks or dirt. Avoid asphalt. Very arid, desert environments will also not work as well for grounding as the flow of electrons is lessened. Go barefoot outside, when possible, for 20-30 minutes or more a day.
2. **Earthing bed sheets.** Purchase high quality earthing bed sheets to connect your body to the Earth while you sleep. In studies, people who sleep on earthing bed sheets are shown to have better sleep quality, less chronic pain, less muscle stiffness, and a greater sense of well-being.
3. **Earthing shoes.** For when you can't go barefoot outside, you may consider wearing earthing shoes. A copper wire in the sole of the shoe conducts the Earth's negatively charged electrons into your body.

Grounding Meditation

This grounding meditation will help you return to calm, and reconnect with the stability of the Earth.

- Find a quiet, protected space where you will remain undisturbed for 20 minutes. If possible, go outside and let your bare feet connect with the Earth's surface. If inside, consider standing on an earthing mat.
- Begin by stand with your bare feet shoulder-width apart, toes pointed forward and spread slightly apart.
- Focus on your breath moving in and out of your body.
- Feel the soil or grass with your feet. Let them sink into the ground. They are connected to the Earth. They are a part of the Earth.
- Gently close your eyes.

- Now imagine your breath starting in the soil beneath your feet.
- The Earth's nourishing energy sends breath up through the soles of your feet, up your legs, into your abdomen, and fills your lungs.
- As you breathe in through your feet, imagine a white line connecting your head with the heavens. Your head is effortlessly floating above your spine, and your feet are connected with the ground.
- Breathe. Breathe up from the Earth.
- Roll your hips slightly forward to straighten your spine and bend your knees a small degree.
- Breathe the nourishing energy of the Earth up through your feet into your body.
- Relax the tension in your shoulders. Let your arms hang gently by your sides. Relax your hands.
- Relax your jaw and release any tension in your face. Many of us unknowingly carry tension in our faces and necks.
- Breathe. You are connected with the Earth.
- Your breathing is slow, and relaxed, and requires no effort. Your body is at peace with the Earth, drawing nourishing energy from the Earth's surface.
- Scan your body for any tension. Gently let it unfold. Gently let it go.
- You are here, now. There is nothing to do but be here. To breathe. To let your body be connected to the Earth, drawing breath and calming energy from the Earth.
- Rest in this feeling of groundedness and centeredness.
- Breathe.
- When you feel ready, bring your attention back to your body and slowly open your eyes.
- Thank yourself and the Earth for this time of healing and grounding.

At any time that you feel the need for grounding, visualize your breath rising from the Earth through your feet, and you will feel more centered and calmer.

Grounding is essential for empaths in times of emotional turmoil or stress. If another person's emotional turmoil starts to overwhelm you, you can combine shielding and grounding as an exceptional protective measure.

CHAPTER 5: STEP 2: HOW TO BUILD BETTER BOUNDARIES

We will take a detour from meditation, visualization and grounding and move toward relationships. While Step 1 will help immensely with emotional overload, stress, and self-protection, Step 2 will assist in keeping relationships from a harmful dynamic that is common among empaths – lack of boundaries.

Many empaths have a hard time enforcing boundaries. What exactly are boundaries? They are the limits, or guidelines that you do not want crossed either emotionally or physically in relationships. Boundaries are the behaviors that you accept or reject from others. They define you as separate from other people's needs, wants, desires, feelings, thoughts and actions. Based on this definition, do you see how maintaining boundaries may be difficult for an empath? But boundaries are important because they protect you by letting other people know how to acceptably treat you.

It is often difficult for empaths to separate another person's feelings from their own – especially in close relationships (as seen in the fMRI study in Chapter 1). But having strong boundaries is critical for healthy relationships and your psychological well-being. Boundary erosion can be a result of being an empath, or it can be a result of life-long relationship patterns.

Take a hard look at your relationships and see if you have a pattern of your boundaries being crossed. Strong boundaries are essential. They give protection to your individuality, your body, your feelings, your thoughts, and your self-worth. With intact boundaries your self-respect will increase and your relationships with others will become healthier.

Follow these steps for building healthy boundaries.

1. Introspection – what is okay with you spiritually, emotionally, and physically? On the other hand, what makes you uncomfortable spiritually, emotionally and physically? These are your limits. If someone or something makes you uncomfortable, they are likely crossing your boundaries. Take a moment to write your answers down.

2. Give yourself permission to say no. Often, boundaries are crossed because we fear what will happen if we say no. Give yourself permission to say no. Give yourself permission to set boundaries. When you let your boundaries be crossed in a relationship, you can feel discomfort, resentment, anger, or frustration. This isn't good for you or for your relationships. Allow yourself to set boundaries. This will make your relationships healthier and make you healthier. Take a moment to write down an instance in which you would like to give yourself permission to say no.

3. Let others know when they have crossed a boundary. Empaths sometimes have the expectation that others will be able to read their emotions or minds and know when they are uncomfortable or have had a boundary crossed. This isn't often the case. Let others know when they have

crossed a boundary. Take a moment to write down a time in the past when you let someone know that they crossed a boundary – or could have let someone know that they crossed a boundary.

4. Take care of yourself. When you take care of yourself by practicing self-care, you are better able to recognize what makes you happy or unhappy. You are better able to contribute meaningfully to relationships. You are better able and more willing to maintain boundaries. Write down three ways you can introduce self-care into your days.

5. Become more self-aware. Listen to your body. It can be the first to tell you that you are uncomfortable or that a boundary has been crossed. When you feel that tightness in your chest, or that queasiness in your stomach, check in and take note of what your body is trying to tell you. Take a moment to think about where in your body you most often feel discomfort and write it down.

Boundary setting is a process. For empaths who are easily enmeshed in other people's emotions, or for empaths who have had trouble setting boundaries in their relationships, this can be a difficult step to complete. However, boundary setting will help strengthen relationships and your self-respect. Between another's action and your response is a space to choose (your response). Breathe in that space. In your response lies the freedom from old patterns and a potential for growth.

Here are examples of boundaries that may need to be set:

- Children leaving the house a mess.
- Children entering rooms without knocking.
- Partner not helping with household tasks.
- A night per week for alone time.
- Co-worker coming by your desk and gossiping while you are trying to work.
- Friend constantly complaining about health concerns.
- Friend frequently calling late at night after you are asleep.
- Family routinely asking for money and not paying you back.
- The list is as varied as it is endless. It is only dictated by your personal preferences and your own set ways that you find acceptable to be treated in your relationships.

Take a moment and consider your personal boundaries. Write a few down. Articulating boundaries to yourself can help you enforce them.

Remember, if it makes you uncomfortable or resentful, a boundary has likely been crossed.

Be gentle with yourself while enforcing or building boundaries. This is a lifelong practice and takes patience and *lifelong practice.*

CHAPTER 6: STEP 3: HOW TO REMOVE UNHEALTHY CONNECTIONS

This step builds on the previous two steps: shielding/grounding and boundaries. However, step 3, removing unhealthy connections, may be the most difficult step of all. As mentioned previously, empaths tend to attract people who may take advantage of their natural tendencies.

Many empaths have a strong need to help, hear, or fix the pain of others – be they friends, family, or strangers. Unfortunately, this need to help can be taken advantage of.

It is a gift of the empath to be able to compassionately relate and heal. However, it is a detriment to the empath if these relationships cause them stress, pain, or illness. Or, if the relationships are all take and no give. For your own well-being and health, you can remove unhealthy connections that cause you undue harm. And you can stop taking on the emotional pain and illnesses of others.

The one thing we can change is how we treat ourselves and how we relate to the world. Yet this one thing has the power to change everything.

Reflect and ask yourself:

1. Do I have a subconscious need to be a caretaker? (Yes/No)
2. Do I believe that other people's needs and feelings are more important than my own? (Yes/No)

3. Do I feel responsible for the feelings of others? (Yes/No)
4. Do I feel responsible for the happiness of others? (Yes/No)
5. Do I feel guilty if I put my own needs, health, or well-being in front of others? (Yes/No)
6. Do I feel that I will not be loved if I don't take on others' emotions/needs/feelings and listen/help/soothe them? (Yes/No)

If any of these beliefs are true for you, they may be contributing to placing yourself in unhealthy relationships, or causing emotional exhaustion. Remember, only when you acknowledge your current self can you begin to change. Revisit the detrimental relationships you identified in the first section of this book. These relationships may need firm boundaries put in place. Some of these relationships may need to be stopped.

It is difficult for an empath to end a relationship. The natural inclination of the empath is to help. However, you should not feel guilt for self-protection or self-care.

The following practice will help you to remove unhealthy connections. It is a visualization technique that can be used as many times as needed. This technique can also be used with people you want to keep in your life. It will allow you to have a relationship without taking on the negative emotions or emotional drain previously characterized by the relationship.

Cord Cutting Visualization

Sit in a quiet place and close your eyes.

- Begin by picturing the person and/or situation that is causing you distress.
- Picture a cord that connects you to that person and/or situation. See the color, width, and length of the cord, and where the cord connects to your body.
- Now very gently imagine unhooking the cord from your body. Imagine the cord flying away. Give the cord the intention to get its needs met elsewhere and in other ways.

- It is not welcome back. You are severing this unhealthy connection.
- Imagine the space on your body where the hook was removed from filling with a healing white light. The space is now smooth and free of hooks or cords.
- Repeat this process with any other unhealthy cords you feel attaching you to that person or situation.

This visualization is very powerful in removing unhealthy and unwanted connections from your person and your subconscious mind. It is an effective way for the empath to rid themselves of detrimental energies and emotions. Using this technique can help detach you from unhealthy relationships. It can also help detach unhealthy dynamics in relationships you would like to keep. Repeat this technique as many times as needed in a particular relationship, or situation, until you feel free of the emotional drain.

This technique keeps other people from drawing on you physically and emotionally. It helps you to separate yourself from others and their emotions. It is extremely beneficial for empaths.

CHAPTER 7: STEP 4: HOW TO USE NATURE TO RECHARGE & HEAL

Now that you have worked on shielding, boundaries, and removing unhealthy connections, you can start implementing daily practices to heal and nourish yourself. First, we will look at the healing power of nature.

If you are an empath, then you likely already know the positive effect that nature has on your emotional state. However, I'd like you to take this one step further. Use nature to heal. If you are emotionally overwhelmed, physically drained, chronically ill - use nature to heal.

This is not just an empath secret. Using nature as a healing tool has been written on in medical journals. Patients in hospital settings with a view of nature heal faster than those without a view of nature. In Japan, physicians frequently prescribe "forest bathing" or *shinrin-yoku* for physical ailments.

More than 100 studies have been conducted on shinrin-yoku. They show that forest bathing lowers cortisol levels, lowers pulse and blood pressure, activates the parasympathetic nervous system, and reduces sympathetic nerve activity associated with stress.[6] Simply put, being in nature lowers stress, calms your body and mind, and reduces diseases associated with chronic stress.

6 Park, BJ and Tsunetsugu et al. The physiological effects of Shinrin-yoku (taking in the forest atmosphere or forestbathing): evidence from field experiments in 24 forests across Japan. Environ Health Prev Med. 2010 Jan;15(1):18-26.

Most importantly, for the empath, being in nature grounds you and helps you heal. As an empath, you should spend a minimum of 30 minutes a day in nature (this can include 20-30 minutes or more of grounding).

Enjoy nature through walks, hikes, gardening, outdoor photography, outdoor sports, bird watching, or even sitting on the bench in the park.

Nature Walk Meditation For Empath Healing

- Find a quiet trail, path, or grassy area in a natural setting.
- At the beginning of the walk clear your mind of distractions. Let go of the distractions of the day, and the pull of the past or the future. This is a time for now. This is a time for noticing.
- Begin walking slowly, noticing each separate movement. Your foot lifting. Your body rocking forward. Your foot touching the ground. Your weight shifting and your opposite foot lifting.
- Appreciate the movement of your body.
- Begin to soak in the calmness and peace of the surrounding environment.
- Walk slowly and deliberately.
- Breathe in the fresh air, notice the scents around you – the scent of grass, leaves, flowers, or the soil. Notice.
- Feel the warmth of the sun on your skin, or the coolness of the breeze, or perhaps a chill in the air
- See the beauty of a leaf, a blade of grass, an insect, a spider web.
- Hear a bird song, a cricket, the wind.
- Soak in the calm and the peace surrounding you.
- Breathe in. Breathe out. Be the calm and the peace.
- Notice.
- If your mind wanders, bring it back to concentrating on your steps.
- With your attention focused on walking, on your breath, or on nature, you are immersed in the healing energies of the natural world.

- When you are ready return your attention to your body and your day. Thank yourself and the natural world for its healing.

The nature walk meditation has immense value for empath healing. As little as 5 minutes a week will provide benefit. However, 30 minutes a day will be invaluable.

CHAPTER 8: STEP 5: HOW TO USE MUSIC TO HEAL

Another daily practice that the empath should include in their healing arsenal is music. Music therapy has been used for much of history. Plato wrote about the healing power of music, and ancient cultures around the world used music in healing ceremonies.

Today, music therapy is used for anxiety, depression, dementia, and cancer in hospitals, nursing homes, schools, and private practices. Music *with a strong rhythm or rhythmic beat* effects breathing rate, reduces blood pressure, reduces muscle tension, and increases the rate of release of endorphins (the body's natural pain killers) and dopamine (the brain's natural mood booster).

Calming music is also known to change the brain's predominate waves from beta (stress) to alpha and theta (relaxed). Music has also been shown to help people release repressed negative emotions and painful memories. It is used in hospice settings for grief work, and to help individuals work through traumatic and highly emotional life events.

Empaths tend to take in and *feel* more stress, strong emotions, and pain than others. Stress is related to an increase in illnesses including: Crohn's disease, IBS, heart disease, stroke, diabetes, and cancer.

Healing Music Meditation

Follow these steps to use music as a tool to reduce stress, increase well-being and heal empath emotional overload.

- Select music that has a strong rhythm, calming beat, or music that you associate with a state of well-being. For example: Pachelbel's Canon in D Major, Watermark by Enya, What a Wonderful World by Louis Armstrong, Three Little Birds by Bob Marley, Weightless by Marconi Union, Moonlight Sonata by Beethoven.
- Find a quiet space where you will not be disturbed and start the music.
- Let the music flow through you.
- Visualize a happy moment, or memory: a time in your life when you felt love, joy, and happiness. Hold that memory and associate it with the song.
- Let the feeling of well-being envelope you as you visualize in detail your chosen memory.
- Connect the feeling of well-being with the music.
- Notice your heart rate slowing, your mood lifting, and your stress reducing.
- Repeat this song with the same memory one time a day for two weeks. You are training your subconscious mind to associate this song with a feeling of well-being.
- In the future, whenever you need to feel uplifted, listen to the song you have chosen.

Music can be a powerful tool for empaths. It can be a healing balm to the soul, and bring relief to the deepest of pains.

If you have a particular memory or trauma that is painful, or a situation that is difficult, you can reprogram your brain to have positive associations with that memory or situation using music. This technique is used in music therapy to retrain your brain – move it out of the mental thought grooves (what yogis call samskara) that form repeating psychological habits/impressions/and thoughts – and move it toward new thoughts and healing.

For in-depth healing of painful memories/trauma using music:

- Select a song with a rhythmic beat that you associate with happiness.
- Settle into a quiet place where you will not be disturbed and start the music.
- Bring the painful or intrusive memory to mind. Hold that memory for a few breaths.
- Now, begin to visualize happy or positive events surrounding that person or situation.
- Let the feelings of positivity and happiness flow into you as you listen to the music.
- Allow this activity to reprogram your subconscious mind to associate the painful memory with more positive feelings through music.
- Repeat this process of associating the memory/situation with the positive music and positive memories daily for two weeks. At the end of two weeks the pain of the memory/situation will be lessened and replaced with positive emotions.

Here's an example.

A dear friend's elderly dog recently died of cancer. Every time he thought of his dog he remembered his dog's death and he experienced pain. He used the above technique to help his healing. He selected the song "Red Rubber Ball" by Cyrkle, as it reminded him of his dog's favorite ball. When he started the music, he thought of his dog's death. At first, he felt pain, and the sadness was overwhelming. As the song played, he associated the music with playing fetch with his dog, taking walks with his dog, and petting his dog. Each day he repeated this process. For two weeks he did this. Every time the song played he found that his pain had lessened. At the end of the two weeks, he noticed that when he thought of his dog, instead of immense pain, he felt happier. His immediate memories were not of his dog's death, but of the happiness and joy his dog brought to his life. Music helped him heal.

Please note, grief is a process and the above technique does not need to be used for grief unless you feel ready.

CHAPTER 9: STEP 6: HOW TO USE MINDFULNESS FOR EMPATH PROTECTION

Mindfulness is a powerful and protective step that empaths can incorporate into their day to day activities. The power of mindfulness for the empath cannot be overstated.

Mindfulness is the action of focusing your awareness on the present moment. In mindfulness you fully focus and accept what is happening in that moment. You acknowledge and accept emotions, thoughts, physical sensations, and stimuli. You do not try to hold on to them, or try to push them away, you merely acknowledge them and let them be *as they are.*

How Mindfulness Helps Empaths

- Helps empaths differentiate between their emotions and the emotions of others. *This is essential as empaths can take on the emotions/feelings of others.*
- Helps empaths attune to their physical reaction to emotions. *Noticing your physical reaction can help you know when your boundaries have been crossed, or when a situation is harmful to your well-being.*
- Helps empaths acknowledge and move through/let go of emotions. *By neither pushing emotions away nor holding them tight, empaths can let emotions and energy flow through them rather than stagnating and causing harm.*

- Calms the mind and alleviates stress.
- Helps empaths remain in the present rather than becoming mired in past memories, pain, illness, or emotions. *People with the ADRA2b gene (mentioned in Chapter 1) have a higher likelihood of developing emotional flashbacks from painful events. Mindfulness helps alleviate this.*
- Scientifically proven to reduce stress, anxiety, depression, chronic pain, and risk of illness. A wealth of medical research studies have shown the vast benefits of mindfulness.

You can practice mindfulness at any time throughout the day. When brushing your teeth, when eating lunch, when interacting with others. The key is to *notice*. Notice your thoughts, notice your feelings, notice the sensations. Fully notice and acknowledge. Be in the present moment. Accept your feelings, thoughts and sensations – do not push them away, do not pull them in tight. Just accept and notice. Please note that noticing and accepting are not the same as over-identifying. You can notice and accept pain or illness without over-identifying as that pain or illness. It is merely a part of the tapestry of experience.

As Rumi says "this being human is a guest house." Accept them, invite them in, do not turn them away, yet do not keep them locked in, let them go, every day will bring a new experience.

Daily Mindfulness Meditation

This 3-minute mindfulness meditation can be practiced daily.

- Sit in a comfortable position, in a quiet space where you will not be disturbed.
- Take a moment to settle into your body. Feel your muscles and your weight settling into your bones.
- Find the rhythm of your breath and the rise and fall of your body.
- Gently close your eyes.

- Now feel yourself sinking into your seat. Feel the weight of your body settling and relaxing. Feel your muscles releasing any tension.
- Inhale. Exhale. Notice your breath moving in through your nostrils, and back out.
- Feel your body sinking deeper into your seat.
- Let any thoughts that arise pass through your mind without holding onto them or pushing them away. Let them pass like clouds in the sky. Let them pass like dandelion seeds floating by on the breeze.
- Now begin to notice your feet. Feel the sensations in your feet and in your toes. Feel the weight of your feet on the floor.
- Notice your legs. The bend of your knee. The weight of your thighs pressing into the chair. Notice any sensations in your legs.
- Notice your abdomen. Feel it moving with the breath. Up and down. Notice any sensations in your abdomen. There is no need to change any sensations, only notice and accept them as they are.
- Now, notice your hands and arms. Are they tight? Are they relaxed? Acknowledge the sensations.
- Notice your shoulders and neck. There may be tension here, tiredness. That is okay. Notice the sensations.
- Breathe.
- Notice your face. Notice your jaw. Feel any tightness or pain. Feel any relaxation. Feel the sensations.
- Notice your whole body. The entirety of yourself. The sensation of sitting here, breathing, being – here, now, with you.
- Notice your breath.
- Breathe.
- Notice.
- Thank yourself for this moment of mindful awareness.
- Slowly open your eyes.

Practicing mindfulness daily will help you acknowledge strong emotions and let them *flow through you and out of you.* This is essential for the empath, as empaths tend to take in the emotions of others and hang on to them. Mindfulness is a tool that can help shield the empath from that tendency. It is an essential protective measure. As you have seen, mindfulness can also help empaths heal from strong negative emotions.

CHAPTER 10: STEP 7: HOW TO USE YOUR INTUITION TO PROTECT & HEAL

Empaths have a highly developed intuition. This final step utilizes that gift. As an empath you can trust your intuition to guide you. Your intuition can steer you into healthier relationships, and more beneficial environments.

How Do You Use Intuition?

1. Listen to your body – as the saying goes, "the gut knows". Every person has a unique way that their body responds to harmful or stressful situations. Knowing how your body responds can be helpful in evaluating whether a situation or person is healthy for you.

Here is a list of common "body indicators":

- Clenched jaw
- Headache
- Tight shoulders
- Tight throat
- Tight chest
- Stomach upset/nausea/gut trouble
- Palpitations
- Itchy skin

If you find your "body indicator" is activated by a person or situation, then your body is telling you that you need to take one of the steps (shielding, grounding, boundaries, cutting ties, nature, music, or mindfulness) to protect or heal yourself. Listen to your body, it is often the "canary in the coal mine" and frequently wiser than your conscious mind.

2. Ask for guidance.

If you are unsure in a situation, or unclear about how to address a relationship or a problem you can ask for guidance. Asking for guidance can take two different forms. First, you can ask your wise, compassionate inner-self for the answer. Each of us has a wise inner-self, if you listen closely, that inner-self will have an answer. Second, you can ask a higher power for an answer through prayer or meditation. In both cases, if you are open to hearing an answer, you can receive guidance in understanding which direction to take.

3. Listen to your dreams.

Dreams are the subconscious mind's way of communicating to our waking self. Your subconscious often has the answer to your daily problems. Freud, Jung, and many other psychoanalysts have successfully used dreams to delve into the subconscious mind and solve problems of the conscious self. Use the following method for healing, guiding and gaining greater understanding of yourself through dreams.

- Before going to sleep have a pen and paper next to your bed. Write down on the paper the question you would like your dreams to answer. For example: should I take this job; what should I do about my brother; should I stay in this relationship; should I buy this house?
- As you fall asleep silently repeat your question. Ask yourself to dream the answer and to *remember* your dream. If you gently stroke the back of your hand as you repeat the question it will be absorbed more readily by the subconscious.

- Upon waking, *immediately* write down anything you remember from your dreams. Dreams fade quickly. Write down the details and any emotions you remember feeling during the dream. The emotions felt during a dream sequence are just as important as the places, events, and actions.
- After writing down the dream, you can attempt to translate the dream yourself, or consult a dream dictionary.
- If you do not remember your dreams, repeat the request each night until you feel that a dream has answered your question, or the answer has come to you in another way.

Common Dream Symbols:

Here are a few common dream symbols and dream metaphors to help in your dream analysis.

House: When you dream of a house, you are often dreaming of yourself. The house is a representation of you. The different rooms represent different parts of you. For example, the attic represents your mind.

Water: Water in a dream represents your emotional state. Note whether the water is choppy, calm, murky, or clear. This will help you identify your subconscious emotional state.

People: People in dreams, including family, friends or strangers, often do not represent those individuals, but rather a dominating characteristic of that person. For example, if you dream of your brother, who you think of as adventurous, then you may be dreaming that you need more adventure in your life.

Flying: If you find yourself flying in a dream, it represents a sense of freedom, or the desire for freedom in a particular situation.

Naked: Finding yourself naked in a dream can have many different interpretations. It can mean that you are feeling vulnerable, exposed or misjudged.

You are the best judge as to the meaning of your dreams. The key to interpretation is asking a question of your subconscious, and writing the answering dream down in a dream journal. The answers will come.

CONCLUSION

Thank you for following this journey through the 7 steps for emotional healing, self-protection and building better relationships as an empath. I hope that you have gained a greater understanding and appreciation of yourself. As you use these steps in your life, remember the practice of patience and self-compassion.

In your journey you may also consider exploring these self-care tips:

- **Essential Oils** – Lavender essential oil has been shown to impact the autonomic nervous system by reducing rapid heart rate, reducing stress and anxiety, and regulating blood pressure. It also promotes restful sleep. Place a drop of the essential oil on a cotton ball and inhale.

- **Tea** - Drinking chamomile tea, lemon balm tea, or peppermint tea can help soothe frayed nerves.

- **Animals** – Owning a pet has been shown to make people healthier, happier, and longer lived. A dog, cat, or other animal companion can be extremely soothing for an empath or highly sensitive person.

- **Acupuncture** – Acupuncture is approved by the World Health Organization as a treatment for many chronic illnesses and mental health diagnoses including stress, anxiety, depression, and PTSD. If you have experienced an emotional trauma, or need help managing stress and anxiety, acupuncture has been proven to be more effective or just as effective as medication or cognitive behavioral therapy in many medical studies.

- **Exercise and Diet** – As yogis of the past taught, a healthy body creates a healthy, happy mind. By giving your body the gift of exercise and healthy food, you are providing it fertile soil for emotional and mental well-being. Exercise helps clear stagnant energy and boosts mood. Try cutting out caffeine, excess alcohol, refined flours, and white sugar. A whole-food diet is best.

- **Don't overload your schedule** – As any empath or highly sensitive person can attest, being out amongst people and doing too much is emotionally draining. Do not overbook yourself. It is okay to schedule in time for rest, relaxation, and renewal.

- **Practice Mindful Self-Compassion** – Again, give yourself the gift of self-compassion. When a friend or loved one is struggling, empaths freely provide them with loving compassion. You too are worthy of compassion. Instead of being hard on yourself when you struggle or fail, give yourself the great gift of self-compassion.

  o A wonderful exercise in self-compassion is a compassionate touch. When you find yourself stuck in self-judgment, or feeling overwhelmed give yourself a gentle, soothing touch. Place your hand over your heart. Feel the weight and warmth of your hand on your chest. Let your hand rest there and make small circles. Let your body respond to your own caring, soothing touch. Know you can give yourself physical comfort whenever you need. Try other places, such as cradling your cheek, cupping your hands together, or rubbing your arm. Just as you would hug a small child, you can hug yourself with a compassionate touch.

- **Crystals** – Crystals have been used for centuries as an aid for healing and protection. Empaths can make excellent use of any number of crystals. Be sure to buy your crystals from a reputable source and cleanse them before use. You can cleanse crystals by placing them in the sun from dawn until dusk, or for a minimum of 4 hours.

- **Selenite:** Selenite has a high energy vibration and is able to clear away negative energy and blockages. It has an amazing ability to purify and cleanse. If you ever feel that negative energy is "sticking" to you, you can use selenite to clear it away. Use a selenite wand by passing it over your body to cleanse away any negative energy clinging to you. You can also wear selenite jewelry. However, because of selenite's high vibrational energy you will also want to wear a grounding stone, such as black tourmaline.

- **Black tourmaline:** As selenite has such a high vibration, it is useful to use it in conjunction with a grounding stone like black tourmaline. Black tourmaline is a powerful grounding stone and through the centuries has also been used as protection against negative energies and destructive thoughts. It is one of the best stones for protection, and keeps negative energies from attaching to you. Black tourmaline and selenite are a powerful duo of cleansing and protection stones for empaths.

- **Black Kyanite:** Similar to black tourmaline, black kyanite is an excellent protection stone. It is frequently used in conjunction with cord cutting meditations, as black kyanite is said to sever unhealthy, negative connections.

- **Amethyst:** Amethyst is one of the best go-to, all-purpose crystals that an empath can have. An empath can carry an amethyst on them at all times for the benefits of healing, protection, and stress-relief. It is a wonderful and gentle crystal.

- **Citrine:** Citrine is a sunny, positive stone that brings light and happiness. Citrine is wonderful for children who are empaths. They gravitate toward its light and happy nature. When they feel upset or are leaning toward a tantrum, a handful of citrine can help re-align their emotions and bring back their sunshine. You can teach a child to meditate on the sunniness of citrine to help them during difficult moments. Many children gravitate to rocks and crystals and citrine is one of the best.

You can search the world over and not find anyone as deserving of care and compassion as yourself. All the best on your journey.

Final Note

A Warm Thank You

Thank you for reading this book and for bringing your light to the world.

I hope that you have found value in these 7 steps towards healing, self-protection and building better relationships. You are a blessing to this world.

-Suzanne Evans

Made in the USA
Middletown, DE
17 December 2019